PANORAMAS

OCEAN LIFE

BackPACK**BOOKS**

○

NEW YORK

CONTENTS

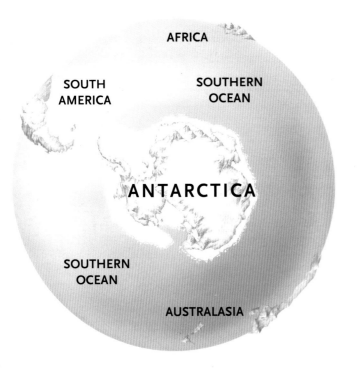

SOUTHERN OCEAN

The Southern Ocean surrounds the continent of Antarctica. More than half of this ocean freezes over each winter. Icebergs, which break off from the Antarctic icecap, float among the sea ice.

THE OCEANS

OCEAN WATERS cover nearly three-quarters of our planet's surface. There are five great oceans: in order of size, the Pacific, Atlantic, Indian, Southern, and Arctic Oceans.

SURFACE WATERS

MANY BIRDS catch their food from the surface waters of the ocean. The tropic-bird and booby plunge into the water itself. Air trapped in the feathers of these diving birds enables them to rise to the surface quickly and fly away with their catch. Other ocean birds, such as the albatross, snatch fish from the surface with their beak or claws.

Some creatures live half above and half below the water. The upper part of a Portuguese man-of-war is like a sac of air. It floats on the surface, dragging its tentacles below the water, trapping small fish.

RED-TAILED TROPICBIRD

PORTUGUESE MAN-OF-WAR

WANDERING ALBATROSS

BROWN BOOBY

OYSTERCATCHER

BLUE-FOOTED BOOBY

FLYING FISH

BANDED SEA SNAKE

GREEN TURTLE

STINGRAY

PORTUGUESE MAN-OF-WAR

SHORE CRAB

FLOUNDER

Sea level

Depth 15 ft.

CORAL REEF

Coral can grow in shallow waters along tropical coasts around the world. Sometimes it forms great underwater banks, called coral reefs. Coral comes in many fantastic shapes and colors. Many colorful animals live on or near the reefs. Some fish, such as the parrotfish, use their markings to identify others of their own species.

KEY

1 Starfish
2 Zebra lionfish
3 Damselfish
4 Sea horse
5 Parrotfish
6 Angelfish
7 Barracuda
8 Clownfish
9 Butterflyfish
10 Pufferfish
11 Moray eel
12 Leopard shark

OCEAN DEPTHS

MOST ocean life is located near the surface, where sunlight can easily pass through the water, allowing plankton (tiny plants) to grow. Many animals feed on plankton. Below 700 feet only a little light can get through—fewer animals live here. Some of these creatures travel to and from the surface to feed.

Depth
30 ft.

Depth
300 ft.

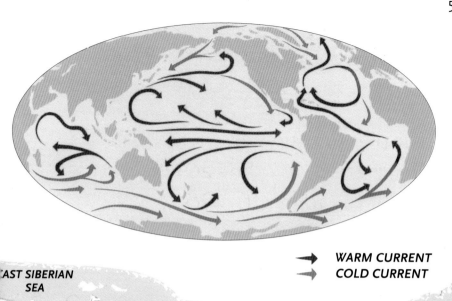

OCEAN CURRENTS

The ocean waters swirl around the Earth. Heated by the sun, surface waters flow from the warm tropics toward the icy polar regions. As they do so, colder currents move in to take their place. Winds that blow over these ocean currents carry their warm or cool temperatures to the nearby lands. The Gulf Stream, which flows north from the Gulf of Mexico, brings mild, wet weather to northwestern Europe.

→ **WARM CURRENT**
→ **COLD CURRENT**

EAST SIBERIAN SEA

BAFFIN BAY

SEA OF OKHOTSK

BERING SEA

HUDSON BAY

NORTH AMERICA

ATLANTIC OCEAN

PACIFIC OCEAN

GULF OF MEXICO

CARIBBEAN SEA

SOUTH AMERICA

AUSTRALASIA

MAGNIFICENT FRIGATEBIRD

BOTTLENOSE DOLPHIN

FLYING FISH

ZOOPLANKTON

PLANKTON

OCEAN FLYERS AND LEAPERS

Flying fish skim the surface of the water, gliding for distances of up to 350 feet. Their "wings" are actually long, taut fins. They fly to escape predators in the water, making them a target for birds.

Many whales and dolphins leap out of the water. This is known as breaching. Some smaller kinds can go very high and often perform somersaults while they are in the air.

PLANKTON

The plants of the ocean are not like those on land. Called plankton, they are microscopic in size and float around in the sunlit waters. Microscopic animals, called zooplankton, feed on them. The most common kind of zooplankton are tiny shrimplike animals called copepods. The young of fish and crabs are also kinds of zooplankton.

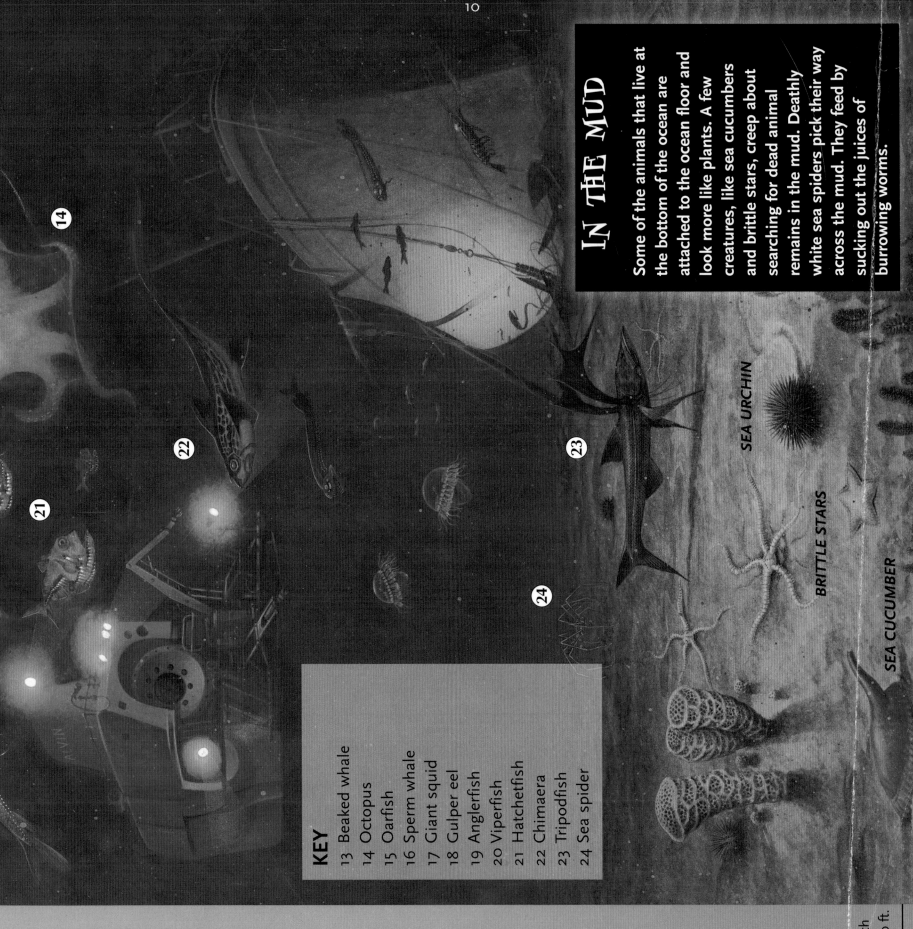

IN THE MUD

Some of the animals that live at the bottom of the ocean are attached to the ocean floor and look more like plants. A few creatures, like sea cucumbers and brittle stars, creep about searching for dead animal remains in the mud. Deathly white sea spiders pick their way across the mud. They feed by sucking out the juices of burrowing worms.

SEA URCHIN

BRITTLE STARS

SEA CUCUMBER

KEY

13 Beaked whale
14 Octopus
15 Oarfish
16 Sperm whale
17 Giant squid
18 Gulper eel
19 Anglerfish
20 Viperfish
21 Hatchetfish
22 Chimaera
23 Tripodfish
24 Sea spider

Depth
15,000 ft.

CHAMPION DIVER

The sperm whale is known to dive deeper than 3,000 feet, but it can probably go to depths of more than 9,000 feet in search of its favorite prey, giant squid. The sperm whale can spend up to two hours underwater before returning to the surface to breathe.

DEEP-SEA CREATURES

Below about 10,000 feet, the water is as black as night and icy cold. How do animals survive at this depth? A steady supply of food rains down from above in the form of decomposing parts of dead animals and plants. Scavengers living in deep waters feed on these remains and other animals feed on them. Some creatures, like the hatchetfish or lanternfish, travel to the upper layers of the ocean to feed and may be snapped up as food themselves on the way back down. Many deep-sea animals can create light, a feature known as bioluminescence.

Depth 3,000 ft.

Depth 10,000 ft.

POLAR WATERS

THE WATERS of the Arctic Ocean are among the coldest in the world. Some ocean animals migrate to warmer places in winter. Others stay and try to find enough food to survive until spring.

The walrus is well equipped for life in such a freezing climate. Its massive body is covered with tough skin. Underneath, there is a thick layer of fat, called blubber, that protects the animal from the cold. The bearded seal, named for the long bristles on its snout, stays in the Arctic all year round. It feeds on the fish and shellfish it finds on the seabed.

UNICORN OF THE SEAS

The narwhal, a kind of whale, is one of the strangest-looking creatures in Arctic waters. The males have a spiraling tusk that is actually one of their two teeth. They may use it as a sword to fight other males to win females. Narwhals feed on squid, shrimp, crabs, and fish.

WALRUS

N GIANTS

NS are home to the giants
nal kingdom: the whales.
ports their enormous
g them to move freely in
. With their long, sleek
ippers, and tails, some
uite similar to fish,
arks. They are not fish at
out mammals. Like
must breathe air, they are
, and the mothers nurse
hey belong to a group of
ed the cetaceans (the
ludes dolphins and

porpoises). The cetaceans are the only
mammals to spend their entire lives in
the water. Instead of thick coats of hair
to keep them warm,
they have thick
layers of fat, called
blubber, beneath
their skins. The
largest animal
on Earth is the
blue whale. A
fully grown blue
whale can measure
more than 100 feet.

PACIFIC OCTOPUS

Arm span up to 30 feet
Octopuses have eight sucker-
covered arms, which they use
to clamber about the ocean
floor—and occasionally
swim—in search of crabs and
lobsters to eat.
They seize their
prey in
their suckers, stun it with
venom, and then crush it in
their powerful beaks.
Octopuses use their
intelligence and keen eyesight
both to hunt and avoid
capture. They can also change
color, squirt ink, and make a
quick getaway by jetting water
through their bodies.

PACIFIC OCTOPUS

WHY DO WHALES SING?

Whales can make different sounds to express
anger, sadness, and surprise. There is
evidence that they sing to locate their position
in the ocean and also to communicate with
one another. They sing new songs each year
and may also sing songs that they have
picked up from other whales.

MANTA RAY

30 feet wide
Skates and rays are relatives of
sharks. The largest of the ray family,
the manta, is dark gray or black on its
topside and white on its
underside. It swims by
flapping its huge
"wings," often at
great speed. It
can even leap
out of the
water!

All animals are drawn to scale.

LEATHERBACK TURTLE

6 feet long
The leatherback turtle's black
shell feels like hard rubber. The
largest marine turtle, its front
flippers have a span of about
20 feet. It is also the deepest-
diving reptile in the world,
capable of reaching depths of
3,000 feet or more.

LEATHERBACK TURTLE

POLAR BEAR

BEARDED SEAL

NARWHAL

BELUGA
WHALE

POLAR BEAR

The polar bear is the largest member of the
bear family. Adult bears roam the ice alone,
and often swim from one area of ice to
another. Strong claws and hairs on the soles of
their feet give them a good grip on the slippery
ice. The bears' thick fur keeps them so warm
that they sometimes have to jump into the
freezing water to cool off!

With their white coats, polar bears are well
camouflaged in the snow and ice. This is
particularly useful for the hunting of seals.
Bears sometimes take seals by surprise as they
rest on the ice. They also hunt by lying silently
in wait at a breathing hole, grabbing the seal
as its head pops up to take a breath.

WHITE WHALE

The beluga whale is born dark gray, but turns
white by the time it is 10 years old. It is known
for its songs, including clicks, squeaks,
whistles, and mooing sounds. Its enemies are
killer whales and polar bears.

AMAZING OCEAN CREATURE

Many ocean creatures may look
extraordinary to us, but the colors,
shapes, or other distinctive features they have
are there to help them survive. Their sharp
spines or powerful venom, for example, may
give them protection against predators—or
equip the animals to be dangerous predators
themselves.

POISONOUS CR

Jellyfish are more than 95% w
heart, bones, brain, or even r
venomous creature on Earth
Just a touch of its powerful
stinging tentacles can
kill a person in four
minutes. The largest
jellyfish, the lion's
mane, has tentacles
more than
150 ft. long.

COWFISH

The thornback cowf
like a tank! Its body
box with holes for it
fins. Its skin is h
horns give i

LIONFISH

The zebra lionfish *(above)* may
look very beautiful, but those
spiny fins are deadly to touch.
Each fin contains enough lethal
venom to kill its prey. Lionfish
hunt in groups, sometimes
herding smaller fish together.

SHARK

...feeds on fish, turtles, and sea mammals. It has up to 3,000 teeth in its mouth, arranged in rows. Some are 3 inches long and serrated—perfect for biting large chunks of flesh out of a dolphin or sealion.

...is one of ...redators ...gh it has ...and kill ...it usually

BLUE WHALE

Up to 100 feet long

A blue whale is the largest whale of all. A fully grown blue whale's heart can be as big as a small car, and its tongue can weigh more than an elephant! Their huge size made blue whales a prime target for whale hunters. By 1967, their numbers had dropped so low that hunting blue whales was banned. Even today, their numbers remain very low, and they are still in danger of extinction.

Like all whales, the blue breathes air, so it must come to the water's surface from time to time. While it is submerged, the whale's nostrils, or blowholes, remain shut. When it comes to the surface, it breathes out in an explosion of waste air and water droplets known as a "blow" or a "spout."

GREAT WHITE SHARK

DIVER

BLUE WHALE

A GIANT APPETITE

The blue whale spends its summers in the cold waters around the Arctic icecap or Antarctica. It feeds on huge quantities of tiny shrimplike animals called krill. To satisfy its huge appetite, it engulfs about 40 million of them each day. Like all baleen whales, the blue whale has hundreds of baleen plates, each fringed with stiff hairs hanging from its upper jaw. It uses them as a kind of sieve, trapping the krill from great gulps of seawater. In winter, the blue whale heads for tropical waters, where it mates.

SOUTHERN ELEPHANT SEAL

ARK

...RK

...e world's ...ying ...aters, it

feeds on krill and fish that it filters from the water passing through its gills. Although it has thousands of tiny teeth, it never uses them.

DIVER

Scuba divers can only dive to about 150 ft. below the surface of the ocean. Below that, the water pressure is too high.

ELEPHANT SEAL

Up to 20 feet long

Elephant seals are named for their huge size and the male's elephantlike "trunk." The female is much smaller than the male.

STRIPED BURRFISH

The striped burrfish (right) hunts for shellfish, barnacles, and crabs to eat. It uses its spines for defense. If a bigger fish threatens to eat it, the burrfish immediately swallows huge mouthfuls of water and blows itself up to the size of a soccer ball, with its spines sticking out in all directions. It is not such a tasty-looking meal!

PIPEFISH

The harlequin ghost pipefish (above) is covered in bony plates. This relative of the sea horse is camouflaged to look like a piece of coral, making it difficult to spot by attackers. It feeds on zooplankton and shrimps, which it sucks in through its tubelike mouth.

SEA SLUG

Unlike its land relatives, the sea slug (right) is very brightly colored. But be warned, this animal is deadly poisonous! The delicate tufts on its back are the stinging parts that once belonged to a jellyfish or sea anemone. The sea slug devours these creatures, then borrows their stinging parts for its own use.

STARFISH

The starfish (above) has neither head nor brain. Its mouth is in the center of its body. Its spiny skeleton is on the outside. The starfish creeps slowly along the seabed in search of its prey. Using the suckers on its arms, it fastens on to a tightly closed clamshell and gradually pries it open. Then the starfish feeds on the fleshy parts inside.

OCEAN TRAVELERS

ANIMALS are always on the move in search of fresh sources of food. Some travel at the same time each year to places where the new season brings a more favorable climate for feeding or breeding. This is called migration. Journeys of migration are sometimes made to distant parts of the world. The most ambitious travelers may fly or swim incredible distances across oceans and back again to the same places each year.

ARTIC TERN

The Arctic tern (right) breeds in the Arctic when it is summer in the North. Then it flies 8,000 miles to spend the souther summer feeding in Antarctic wate Over the course of its life, it may more than 600,000 miles.

GREEN TURTLE

Probably the farthest-traveled reptile is the green turtle (above). Every two or three years, it swims up to 1,400 miles from the waters off the coast of Brazil, where it feeds, to its breeding grounds on tiny Ascension Island in the middle of the Atlantic Ocean.

EELS

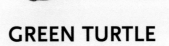

The young of the European eel (above) are born in the Sargasso Sea, east of Florida. They spend the next few years drifting across to Europe, where they swim up rivers to grow into adults.

ARCTIC TERN

YOUNG OF EUROPEAN EEL

ATLANTIC OCEAN

GREEN TU

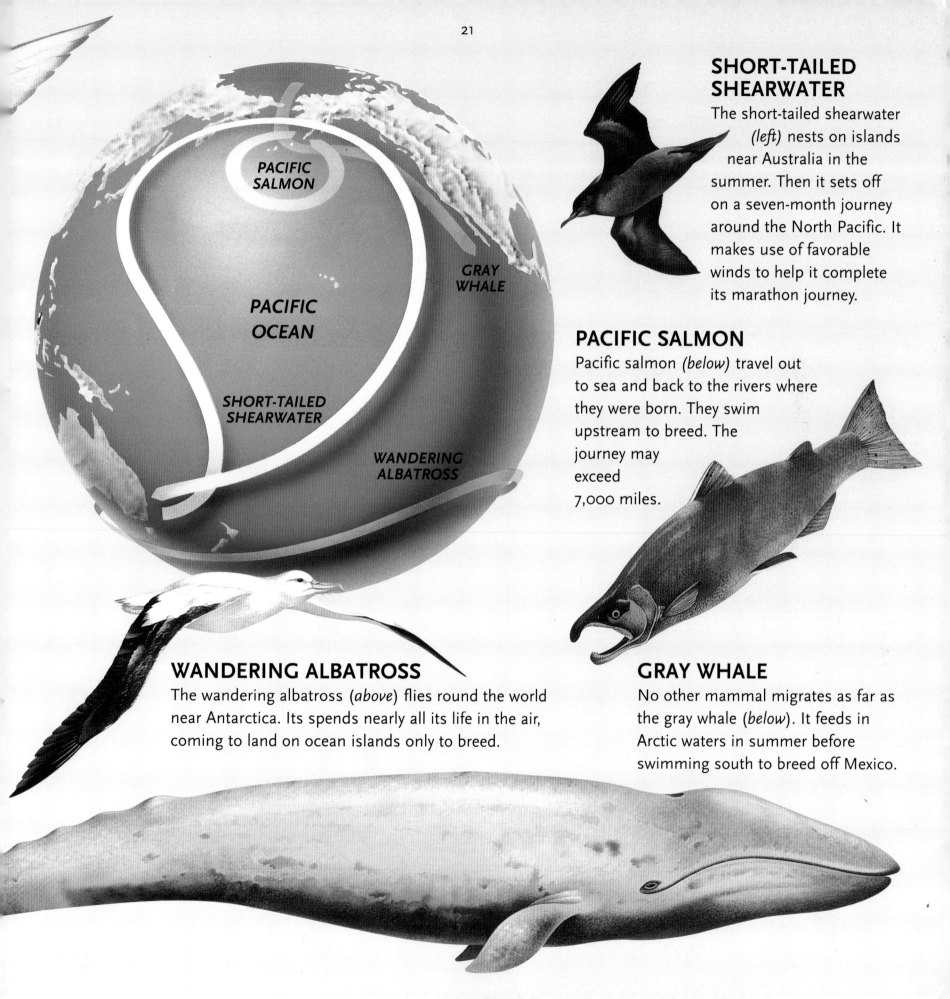

PACIFIC
SALMON

PACIFIC
OCEAN

GRAY
WHALE

SHORT-TAILED
SHEARWATER

WANDERING
ALBATROSS

SHORT-TAILED SHEARWATER

The short-tailed shearwater (*left*) nests on islands near Australia in the summer. Then it sets off on a seven-month journey around the North Pacific. It makes use of favorable winds to help it complete its marathon journey.

PACIFIC SALMON

Pacific salmon (*below*) travel out to sea and back to the rivers where they were born. They swim upstream to breed. The journey may exceed 7,000 miles.

WANDERING ALBATROSS

The wandering albatross (*above*) flies round the world near Antarctica. Its spends nearly all its life in the air, coming to land on ocean islands only to breed.

GRAY WHALE

No other mammal migrates as far as the gray whale (*below*). It feeds in Arctic waters in summer before swimming south to breed off Mexico.

GLOSSARY

BALEEN A material that grows as plates from the roof of the mouth in some kinds of whale. It is sometimes known as "whalebone." The plates are fringed with fibers, and they are designed to filter plankton from seawater.

BIOLUMINESCENCE The production of light by living things. It enables deep-sea fish to locate one another for mating or to attract their prey.

CAMOUFLAGE The means by which living things escape the notice of predators (or prey, when they themselves are predators) by using their colors or patterns to blend into the surroundings.

CETACEANS An order of mammals that includes the whales, dolphins, and porpoises. The cetaceans can only live in water—either in the ocean or large rivers—but, because they are mammals, they must come to the surface to breathe. They are streamlined animals, and have almost no hair.

CORAL A hard substance produced by polyps, tube-shaped animals with a mouth at one end surrounded by a ring of tentacles. The polyps, which live together in large numbers or colonies, are encased in a limestone skeleton, which is the coral. When they die, new polyps grow in their remains, and produce more coral. Eventually a large bank, or coral reef, is built up.

GILLS The breathing organs of fish and some other water creatures that extract oxygen from the water.

INVERTEBRATES Animals without backbones. They include insects, spiders, shellfish, worms, and sponges.

MIGRATION The movement of a population of animals from one place to another at a certain time of the year, to feed or breed.

OCEAN The body of salt water that covers about 71% of the Earth's surface. It is divided into the Pacific, Atlantic, Indian, Southern, and Arctic Oceans.

PLANKTON Animals and plants that live near the surface of the ocean. They drift freely in the ocean currents. Minute plants, for example, algae, are kinds of plankton. They are eaten by tiny animals, called zooplankton. These animals are in turn eaten by larger animals, from tiny fish to enormous whales.

SCAVENGER An animal that feeds on the remains of food killed by other animals.